PORTSMOUTH

BETWEEN THE WARS

ANTHONY TRIGGS

HALSGROVE

First published in Great Britain in 1998
Reprinted 2000

British Library Cataloguing in Publication Data

A CIP record for this book is available from the British Library

ISBN 1 874480 03 1

HALSGROVE
Halsgrove House
Lower Moor Way
Tiverton
Devon EX16 6SS
Tel: 01884 243242
Fax: 01884 243325
www.halsgrove.com

Printed in Great Britain by Bookcraft (Bath) Ltd, Midsomer Norton

Acknowledgements

I must thank Geoffrey Elliott, editor of *The News*, Portsmouth, for permission to use pictures from the newspaper's collection. My colleagues June Long and Carol Farr also deserve thanks for uncomplainingly allowing me to be a regular nuisance in the photographic department and the newspaper's library. My old friend Tom Dethridge came up trumps with some images from his extensive transport collection, and Alan King and his ever-helpful staff in the local studies department of the Portsmouth Norrish Central Library have been a great help with checking references. And as always I give my thanks to my wife Sue, whose help, encouragement, and good ideas are always there.

Introduction

Portsmouth, like so many towns and cities in the British Isles, was left with huge scars after the First World War. They were not visible scars, but those of suffering and bereavement, as almost a whole generation of young men was wiped out during those terrible years. It was said there was hardly a street or road in the city where no one was in mourning.

Externally Portsmouth suffered not at all, its one and only air raid remaining just a memory. On the night of 25 September 1916, heavy firing by the town defences had set residents' windows rattling, and many left their beds to find out what was happening. High in the air over the dockyard, highlighted by the searchlights, was the long silver shape of a Zeppelin, sliding silently towards Portsmouth from the direction of the Isle of Wight.

The guns were unable to bear upon the airship and the flak was falling short of the target, and she was able to drop two bombs, both of which fell into the harbour. The first exploded near HMS *Victory*, and the second quite close to HMS *Renown*. The airship turned away, gained height, and was soon lost to the searchlights.

Portsmouth had had a narrow escape, for the Zeppelin was the *L31*, commanded by Heinrich Mathy. A man to whom failure was anathema, Mathy was regarded as greatest airship commander of the war.

Mathy wrote in his subsequent report that he had reached Dungeness on his way to London, but considered that the night was too bright for a raid on the capital, so instead turned westwards to Portsmouth.

He was carrying thirty high-explosive bombs and thirty incendiaries. Over the harbour he was blinded by the searchlights and decided to drop his full complement of bombs, as he thought, on the town. But his misjudgement saved Portsmouth, for the other forty-eight must have hit the water without exploding.

After the devastating war – the war to end all wars – Portsmouth settled itself down to getting back to normal, or as near normal as possible in a country hit by unemployment, rising costs and a lack of proper housing. Lloyd George's vision of 'a fit country for heroes to live in' was sadly not to be. Nevertheless Portsmouth embarked on its own programme of slum clearance, shearing away many of the disease-ridden Portsea back-to-backs and replacing them with purpose-built blocks of flats, such as those in Curzon Howe Road.

The council also built estates of council houses – Wymering and Paulsgrove – and private housing spread in areas such as Highbury, where some 3500 homes were planned.

The slump of 1921 left two million jobless, and although unemployment in the relatively prosperous South was bad, it was nothing like the hardships endured in the North-East.

At the end of the Great War Portsmouth dockyard was employing some 23,000 men. With the advent of peace many were laid off and by 1921 the total workforce was down to 9000.

However, in the second half of the 1920s shipbuilding revived and a number of vessels were put on the stocks, including a trio of cruisers. In the 1930s the government turned its attention to greater defence, and fleet modernisation and maintenance provided work for the yard.

Entertainment and leisure became increasingly important. The craze for dancing swept the country, the embryonic radio service was coming of age, and cinemas proliferated as film-making took off. In the Portsmouth of the 1930s there was as many as thirty 'picture palaces' in operation.

With the opening of the city airport in 1932, and the electrification of the main London to Portsmouth railway line, travel became easier and Portsmouth's holiday trade increased, bringing more jobs for casual workers.

But by the mid-1930s the raffish atmosphere had waned, the threat of war was growing, and after 1939 the face of Portsmouth was never to be the same.

Germany brought the battle to the skies over the city and the Luftwaffe did not discriminate about where the bombs fell. Countless buildings – historic, old, and new – fell victim to the airborne fire, and the face of a grand old lady under-went a change as whole streets disappeared from the Portsmouth map.

In this collection I have tried to open a window into the peaceful years between the wars, a period often ignored by the compilers of pictorial histories. So queue here for your ticket to an illustrated journey into the past, a nostalgia trip which can be enjoyed without leaving your seat by the fireside.

Anthony Triggs,
Portchester, 1998

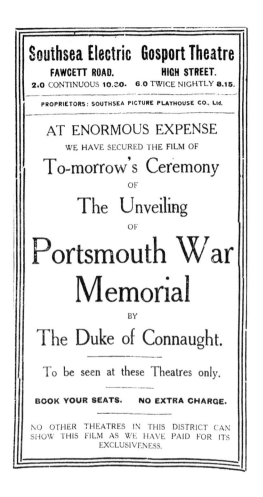
The war to end all wars was over and England was at peace. However, that peace had been bought with the greatest ever sacrifice of human life. Towns and cities nationwide were remembering the fallen in various ways. In Portsmouth the beautiful memorial next to the town hall was unveiled on 19 October 1921, and an estimated 30,000 people gathered in the square to watch the Duke of Connaught perform the emotive ceremony. Two cinemas in the area, the Southsea Electric and the Gosport Theatre, made a scoop by securing the rights to screen the film of the event.

Armistice Day is commemorated on Tuesday, 11 November 1930 on the steps of the Guildhall. The service, led by the Lord Mayor of Portsmouth, Councillor Walter Gleave, attracted a huge crowd. More than 25,000 people packed into the Guildhall Square and paid tribute to fallen comrades and family members. The Last Post was sounded and a single gun was fired in nearby Victoria Park.

The Guildhall with its distinctive minarets is seen here from Victoria Park. This imposing building was opened by the Prince and Princess of Wales in 1890. After the destruction of the war the Guildhall was rebuilt, to be reopened by HM the Queen on 8 June 1959.

The ornate 1600-seat main hall in the Guildhall is pictured in pre-war days before German bombs took their toll on the night of 10 January 1941. The building was left as a shell and the ornate fittings, the beautiful portraits that lined the walls of the upstairs gallery, the organ, and the statuary were all lost for ever.

High in the tower of the Guildhall is the mechanism that drives the four faces of the clock. Here a council worker is giving the complicated system a regular check.

Under a clear blue sky, crowds gather outside the Guildhall as the Prince of Wales (later Edward VIII) arrives to receive the freedom of the newly-created city on 23 July 1926. The prince travelled from the Isle of Wight aboard the destroyer HMS *Winchester*, passing ships decorated for the occasion. After a tour of Southsea in a red open-topped Crossley car the prince was entertained to an all-British lunch at the Guildhall by the Lord Mayor, Councillor Frank Privett, and city dignitaries. The freedom ceremony itself took place in the afternoon. That day the *Evening News*, in a display of patriotic fervour, was printed in ink of royal purple.

The Lord Mayor of Portsmouth, Councillor Frederick Spickernell, welcomes King George VI and Queen Elizabeth, together with the young Princess Elizabeth, to Portsmouth on 19 May 1937. The royal party was visiting the city before embarking aboard the *Victoria and Albert* to review the ships at Spithead in honour of the coronation. (*The News*, Portsmouth)

Although the real warships were anchored at Spithead for the review, Portsmouth had its own vessel, HMS *Coronation*. Made of wood and plaster and built over the old tram shelter, she stood firmly anchored to the Guildhall Square. (*The News*, Portsmouth)

Searchlights criss-cross the night sky as the 1937 Coronation Review ships switch on their illuminations. This picture was turned into an extremely popular postcard by the Portsmouth firm of Mills and Co.

Thousands gathered in the Guildhall Square on 6 May 1939 to see King George VI and Queen Elizabeth depart for Canada and the United States. They arrived on the royal train accompanied by the two princesses, Elizabeth and Margaret. A guard of honour from the 1st Battalion of the King's Own Scottish Borderers assembled in the square, and the route from the town station was lined by Royal Marines from Eastney Barracks. The royal couple then went on to the dockyard, where they embarked aboard the *Empress of Australia*. They returned to England on 22 June, when they were met by the two princesses.

A sea of expectant faces: children crowd the barrier outside the Guildhall, waiting to cheer the royal party as they arrive at Portsmouth on their way to Canada.

The battle cruiser HMS *Hood* leaves Portsmouth watched by spectators at Old Portsmouth. The 42,000-ton vessel was lost in 1941 when she took a direct hit during the epic battle to sink the German battleship *Bismarck*.

A few interested onlookers wait on the beach at Sally Port as the huge bulk of the German cruiser *Leipzig* slides past the Round Tower on her way into Portsmouth Harbour on 11 July 1934. The giant vessel, which was on a visit with the cruiser *Konigsberg*, was the flagship of Rear Admiral Hans Kolbe. She lay alongside at the South Railway Jetty for four days and the city made her officers and crew welcome, little knowing that within a few years their two countries would be at war.

Early on the morning of 19 September 1931, the flagship of the Atlantic Fleet, HMS *Nelson*, makes her way through the mist into Portsmouth. She was closely followed by HMS *Hood*. Both vessels were returning to port after the mutiny at Invergordon, in which 12,000 bluejackets had refused to obey orders in a protest over proposed cuts in pay.

The paddle-steamer *Merstone* is admired by holidaymakers on Southsea beach as she nears the shore to pick up passengers. The 342-ton vessel was built for the Southern Railway in 1928 by the Caledon Shipbuilding Company of Dundee. She was a sister ship to the *Portsdown*, which sank after hitting a mine off Southsea in September 1941. *Merstone* survived the war and was eventually sold for scrap in 1952.

The same vessel from an unusual viewpoint: *Merstone* high and dry for cleaning.

Clarence Pier was originally built to serve the Isle of Wight ferry service, and the earliest horse-drawn bus service ran from the town station to the pier. Here a pleasure steamer is moored at the end of the pier waiting for passengers to embark.

A single car negotiates the big dipper at the Clarence Pier funfair in June 1933, as holidaymakers and residents stroll about taking in the sun – although a few mackintoshes are in evidence. (*The News*, Portsmouth)

Grand Parade at Old Portsmouth in its slightly faded pre-war glory. Many of the buildings in this picture were lost in the Blitz, but a few were saved and still retain their historic elegance.

Blacksmith Mr A.E. Baxter and his family stand outside their smithy at Old Portsmouth for a final photograph. The building was due to be demolished as part of the cathedral extension scheme. It was the end of an era as Mr Baxter's great-grandfather had established the business in 1796.

An assortment of vehicles, including a removal lorry from the Portsmouth firm Humphreys, disembark from the Isle of Wight ferry *Fishbourne* at Old Portsmouth. *Fishbourne*, the first drive-on, drive-off ferry, began operating to and from the island in August 1927.

A cyclist studies the plaque on the wall at Sally Port in Old Portsmouth. The gateway led out to the old landing stage from which so many naval heroes left these shores.

The Hot Walls and the old Victoria Pier dominate the foreground of this picture, looking across the mouth of the harbour towards Fort Blockhouse and the Gosport skyline. (The walls are said to have gained their name during the time of the Spithead mutiny, when it was planned that the defences would be used to fire red-hot shot from cannons.)

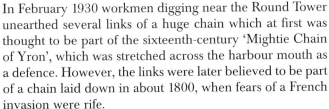

In February 1930 workmen digging near the Round Tower unearthed several links of a huge chain which at first was thought to be part of the sixteenth-century 'Mightie Chain of Yron', which was stretched across the harbour mouth as a defence. However, the links were later believed to be part of a chain laid down in about 1800, when fears of a French invasion were rife.

The old town hall, which stood in High Street, Old Portsmouth, became redundant in 1890 when its replacement, now the Guildhall, was built. The old building, with its stone columns and balcony, became the museum, but sadly was lost in the war along with many historical exhibits. (*The News*, Portsmouth)

The Royal Pier Hotel was an institution in Southsea, catering for the well-to-do traveller. It was originally the Pier Hotel but the name was changed after Queen Victoria stayed there. After the Second World War the hotel was taken over by the army to house service families, and in the 1960s it was converted into student accommodation. It was demolished in 1995 and a new students' hall of residence was built.

Clarence Esplanade and Clarence Pier show up clearly in this fine aerial view postcard by Pan-Aero Pictures of Kingston-on-Thames. The Royal Naval war memorial is in the foreground. It was considerably extended following the losses at sea during World War II.

The naval memorial was unveiled by the Duke of York on 15 October 1924, before an audience of between 25,000 and 30,000 people. Raised by the Imperial War Graves Commission, the memorial commemorates 9700 officers and men of the Portsmouth Port Division who lost their lives but have no known burial place.

Holidaymakers take the air along Clarence Esplanade, Southsea. In the background can be seen the twin turrets of the Esplanade Hotel, a largely wooden structure which was eventually destroyed by enemy action in the war.

This charming picture was picked up at a collectors' fair, and apart from the words 'Portsmouth, August 4th 1932', there is no indication who these day-trippers are or where they have come from in their coaches.

Swimmers and sunbathers get a watery shock as the wash from a passing liner in the Solent forces the water up on to the beach at Southsea. Some hardy souls stay in the water while others hurriedly move their deckchairs higher up the beach.

Time for a tidy-up after a swim at Southsea in this Stephen Cribb picture from the 1920s. 'No bikinis here,' wrote Cribb on the reverse of the print, although these bright young things were no doubt considered daring at the time.

Crowded beaches are not just a phenomenon of today, as this Valentine's postcard clearly shows. The canoe lake is in the middle background, while on the horizon is the clock tower of the Royal Marines Barracks at Eastney.

South Parade Pier, with a ferry boat moored to take on passengers and every seat and deckchair filled on a hot summer day. This was the second pier to be built on the site – the earlier 1879 structure was destroyed by fire in 1904.

The rock gardens at Southsea have always provided a peaceful haven from the summer beach activities. The gardens were designed and laid out by the council in the 1920s when much of the common was purchased by Portsmouth from the War Office.

The bandstand on the common at Southsea offered outdoor dancing during the warm summer evenings. In this postcard view a small crowd has gathered for a Sunday afternoon concert.

The bandstand shown above also became a roller-skating venue. Earlier in the century the skating craze led to rinks being constructed on both Clarence Pier and South Parade Pier, although in those days it was probably a more gentle pastime than the vigorous game of hockey these young men are playing.

The more affluent sun-seekers could avoid the hurly-burly of the beach and rent a corporation sun hut where they could picnic and laze in their deckchairs.

The beach at Southsea is crowded on a glorious day in September 1929. Every eye is turned to the sky as the air race for the Schneider trophy is fought out between Britain and the cream of the Italian Air Force. Flying Officer Richard Waghorn took the prize, having completed the course at an average speed of 328.63 miles an hour. (*The News*, Portsmouth)

The Eastney end of the beach, less genteel than Southsea, was popular with middle-class families. In the background is the area known as 'the tented village' because of its gaily striped corporation-owned bathing tents.

Southsea Castle, seen here from the seaward side, was the venue for the Pageant of Portsmouth, presented by the teachers of the town in 1923. The pageant depicted significant events spanning fifteen centuries of Portsmouth's history. This was the first time the castle had been open to the public for 400 years.

The Old Portsmouth-based printing firm of Charpentier produced this popular postcard depicting the pageant, which ran from 16 to 23 July, with the profits going to the mayor's charities.

Interested spectators watch bowlers on the green at Milton Park. All are smartly dressed, and only a few bare heads can be seen.

On 29 June 1921 Portsmouth councillors took on their Southampton counterparts, not in the council chamber but on the cricket pitch. The game was played at the asylum ground, Milton, and the mayor, Councillor John Timpson, opened the batting. Southampton won the game by 44 runs.

Portsmouth and District Table Tennis League members battle it out in the 1934 championships at South Parade Pier. The Ping Pong Association was formed in 1902, holding championships and tournaments all over the country. In 1921–2 the association was dissolved and re-formed as the Table Tennis Association.

No book on the city would be complete without a reference to Portsmouth Football Club. Pompey's greatest hour was 29 April 1939, when they won the FA Cup with a 4-1 victory over Wolverhampton Wanderers. Here the bus brings the victorious team – and the cup – from Fratton station to an unbelievably crowded Guildhall Square. (*The News*, Portsmouth)

Sunday church parade at the Garrison Church, Old Portsmouth, was always a good subject for the enterprising cameraman, and none was more so than Southsea photographer Stephen Cribb. His pencilled note on the back of this print reads: 'Garrison Church Parade, today, September 1936. Taken near the spot from where I took the same picture 34 years ago.'

The very picture from 1902 mentioned by Cribb shows in graphic detail how fashions, uniforms, and the trees changed in the intervening years!

The beautiful interior of the Garrison Church – sometimes called the Army Cathedral – before the bombs of 1941 did their work. In the raid the roofs of the nave and aisles were lost, but fortunately many of the treasures had been previously removed. The ancient building dates back to the thirteenth century, but was completely renovated in 1866.

Christmas Greetings

St Mark's Church
Portsmouth
Dec. 1920

A bygone Portsmouth place of worship is pictured on this Christmas card from 1920. It shows the old St Mark's Church which stood at the corner of London Road and Derby Road at North End. The church was built in 1874 at a cost of £2,900.

Wymering Methodist Church was opened on 10 February 1937 by the Lord Mayor of Portsmouth, Councillor Frederick Spickernell. The church cost £7,000 to build, and was to be a religious beacon in Wymering, which had only become part of the city in 1920.

The ornate interior of the Kent Street Baptist Chapel is dominated by the array of organ pipes high in the vaulted roof. The chapel replaced an earlier one which was destroyed in 1891, but it too became a victim of wartime bombs.

Decorated trams and buses were a novel way to publicise events in the city, and many were photographed and the pictures subsequently sold as postcards. Top left is a tram festooned with 2024 lightbulbs for Christmas 1933 to help the mayor and corporation wish everyone the season's greetings, while bottom left a card by W.G. & L. Long of the North End Studios shows a tram decorated for the jubilee of George V and Queen Mary. Even the senior service did not lose out: top right is an advertisement for Navy Week. Below, a trolley bus features the coronation of George VI and Queen Elizabeth.

In 1920 Portsmouth Corporation Tramways took delivery of a clutch of new Dennis motor buses, which were used on the Eastney to Alexandra Park and Eastney to Cosham and Drayton services. Here tramways officials pose proudly with the first delivery: fleet number 23, registration TP751.

A mixture of public transport is seen in the view from the roof of a St Helen's Parade property. In the background is the Canoe Lake and beyond that is Lumps Fort, later to be developed as the rose gardens and model village.

Two trolley buses pass one another at Bradford Junction in the late 1930s. The first trolley ran on 4 August 1934. The buses took their power from overhead cables, and were cheap to run, quiet, and pollution-free. The vehicles carried on throughout the Second World War and were eventually phased out in 1963. In the background is the Gaumont, formerly the Plaza cinema with its Art Deco interior, which was turned into a bingo hall in 1965. It closed in 1997 but in 1998 planning permission was granted to the city's Muslim community to convert the listed building into a mosque. (Tom Dethridge)

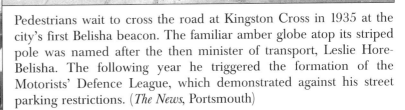

Pedestrians wait to cross the road at Kingston Cross in 1935 at the city's first Belisha beacon. The familiar amber globe atop its striped pole was named after the then minister of transport, Leslie Hore-Belisha. The following year he triggered the formation of the Motorists' Defence League, which demonstrated against his street parking restrictions. (*The News*, Portsmouth)

In 1933 a leader in the *Evening News* read: 'This daring experiment may possibly become historic. Motorists come back from journeys all over England with travellers' tales of winking signs in hundreds of cities and towns.' What was the subject? Portsmouth's first set of traffic lights, which had been erected on the corner of Elm Grove and Grove Road!

Two Thornycroft single deckers wait at the dockyard to take workers to their homes. The two vehicles, fleet numbers 72 and 71, are bound for North End and Alexandra Park.

Borrowers select books at the city's public library in 1935, when it was situated in part of the Technical Institute building behind the Guildhall. The library service had taken residence in the building in 1908, and finally moved to its present purpose-built building in 1976 during the revamp of the city centre.

This view from Park Road shows the Technical Institute, which was opened on 10 September 1908, by the mayor, Ferdinand Foster. The ceremony was preceded by a reception hosted by the mayoress, Foster's daughter Doris, who was just five years old. The institute was built to bring instruction and education to the ordinary person. To the right of the picture can be seen the entrance to Sophia Place.

The Milton branch library in Milton Road was opened in 1925 to help cope with the growing demand for reading matter, using the redundant Congregationalist chapel. The library remained there until the new Beddow Library opened next door.

The ornate interior of Kimbells ballroom in Osborne Road, Southsea, in 1936. A popular venue for dancers before the war, Kimbells continued as a ballroom during the postwar years, but as the popularity of social dancing declined and the pop music culture expanded, it became a club where 'Swinging Sixties' youngsters could see the bands of the day.

On 20 July 1934 a pitifully small fire brigade tackled one of Portsmouth's biggest blazes when the main Co-operative Society store in Fratton Road caught fire. The blaze started in an upstairs room and quickly spread to the rest of the store, and it was reported that within thirty minutes it was impossible to enter any part of the building. Eventually dockyard and naval fire crews helped to contain the blaze. A new building was built on the site and opened in 1937, only to be destroyed by enemy action in 1941. (*The News*, Portsmouth)

Springtime in Milton, looking northwards up Milton Road. Milton was the last of the city's villages and even as late as the 1960s some of the old buildings remained, hidden behind the modern developments.

Bright's Corner at Southsea in the 1930s, looking down Osborne Road, a far more relaxed scene than that of today. On the left is Bright's fashion store, selling all that the lady of the day would require, from bags to umbrellas. The store also ran a circulating library in conjuction with the Times Book Club.

Handleys' corner in about 1925. Founded in 1869, Handleys was a Southsea shopping institution. The store is now part of the Debenhams empire. A Thornycroft bus with its distinctive curving stairs can be seen travelling northwards along Palmerston Road.

The Crown Brewery in Clarendon Street, Landport, in 1932, a sorry sight with its broken windows and missing roof slates. The old building had been sold and was due to be demolished to make way for modern homes.

French onion sellers take to the streets of Portsmouth to sell their wares door to door in 1932. Four boatloads of men and boys arrived from Roscoff, near Brest, in August that year with 50 tons of onions each, but a 10 per cent import tax had just been introduced which made their job all the more difficult.

On 1 January 1931 the motor licensing department moved from its cramped quarters in the Guildhall to the old Portsmouth Grammar School building. The newly implemented Road Traffic Act required motorists to take out a compulsory third-party insurance. It was not until April 1934 that they were compelled to take a driving test!

In 1871 the old 1770 Lion Gate at Portsea was demolished and the pieces were numbered and stored in the dockyard. Later, in 1913, the semaphore tower in the dockyard was destroyed in a mysterious fire, and when it was rebuilt in 1929 the old gate was taken out of storage and built into the base. This picture shows the transformation work nearing completion.

59

Dockyard mateys take a lunch break in their canteen, where a meal and a cuppa could be had at a reasonable price. There was obviously a certain amount of heating: note the iron stove in the foreground.

The imposing gateway to the Portsmouth Naval Barracks – HMS *Nelson*. The barracks were opened in September 1889 and were considered at that time to be the most modern and durable quarters in the country. They were built on the site of the old corporation stone yard and the former Anglesea Barracks. It was said that when the first sailors moved in from their quarters in the hulks in the harbour, as the head of the column was entering the gates, the last files were still tramping along Flathouse Road.

The military homes in London Road, Hilsea, are the same today as they were in this picture, taken before the old cottages on the corner were demolished and the block of shops at Walberant Buildings was constructed. (*The News*, Portsmouth)

The bus depot at London Road, Hilsea, in 1935, looking much as it does today, although the building is now home to the Co-operative Dairies. (*The News*, Portsmouth)

The new entrance to St Mary's Hospital was constructed in 1932 to save patients having to make their way through the tortuous passages of the workhouse. The west wing of the hospital had been the workhouse infirmary, while the east wing was once the infectious diseases hospital.

A nurse keeps close watch on her patients in a ward at St Mary's Hospital. Conditions are spartan but everything looks clean and tidy. Most of the patients are well enough to be allowed to sit up on chairs.

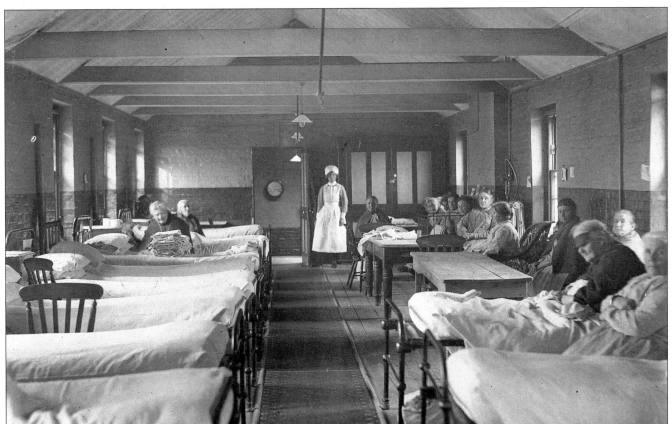

Elderly blind workers make basket-ware at the council's workshops on Portsdown Hill, a facility which attracted representatives from other towns and cities. The city was a leader in the care of the blind, and in 1935 it opened the Jubilee Home for the Blind at Wymering.

Youngsters enjoying the open-air swimming pool at Stamshaw in 1929. The pool was fed from a water tower and was popular among people from the northern part of the city. It closed before the Second World War after remaining derelict for some time.

Built in 1879, Kingston Prison was closed by 1931. However, within a few short years its usefulness was recognised. It was reopened and now houses lifers. Conditions at the prison today are far removed from the spartan regime of the 1930s.

Taken from the Guildhall, this picture gives a clear view of the ornate tram shelter built by the Westminster company of David Rowell. In the background to the right is Russell Street with Buck's tool shop on the corner.

The town station goods yard dominates this scene, taken from the steps of the Guildhall. According to the poster a conducted tour to Wells and Wookey Hole cost 7/3d and one to Salisbury and Stonehenge cost 7/6d.

Workers in the goods yard deal with the many and various items coming through the railway system.

The goods yard being cleared in 1939. The council had purchased the site and the yard moved to new premises at Fratton.

On 1 July 1937, the railway line from Waterloo to Portsmouth was electrified, and at 74 miles it was said to be the longest powered line in the country. Here the special train with the Portsmouth crest on the front is inspected by the Lord Mayor of Portsmouth, Councillor Frederick Spickernell, and other dignitaries.

69

HMS *Fisgard* was the collective name for a cluster of old vessels moored up-harbour and used for the training of artificer apprentices. The vessel on the left is the Boer War veteran cruiser HMS *Terrible*. The training school was finally broken up in 1932 and the vessels were scrapped or moved to new locations. (*The News*, Portsmouth)

Another pair of even older ships, *Implacable* and *Foudroyant*, moored in the harbour. They were used as holiday training facilities by the Society for Nautical Research. *Implacable*, left, was originally the French vessel *Duguay-Trouin* which had been captured at Trafalgar after exchanging fire with HMS *Victory*. After Nelson's flagship went into dry dock *Implacable* held the mantle of the oldest warship afloat. She was brought to Portsmouth in 1932, where she was joined by *Foudroyant*, originally the French vessel *Trincomalee*. *Implacable* finally paid off in 1947 and, in what was considered by many to be an appalling act of vandalism, she was towed out to the Owers lightship and sent to the bottom. As she was leaving harbour the crew of her old adversary, *Victory*, stood to attention. Her partner, *Foudroyant*, remained a familiar sight in the harbour until she was taken to her new home at Hartlepool, where she is undergoing restoration.

Packing cases, boxes, and assorted luggage are unloaded on to the dockside from HMS *Renown* as the Duke and Duchess of York return to Portsmouth on 27 June 1927, after their marathon trip to Australasia. They left Portsmouth on January 6 and during their six-month tour the royal couple travelled 35,000 miles. While in Australia the duke opened the first parliament in the new capital of Canberra. Among the gifts brought home were a number of toys for the young Princess Elizabeth, and a parrot in a cage!

A long line of visitors queue to go aboard HMS *Victory* during the August 1931 Navy Week. In front of *Victory* three submarines are laying alongside – *L16*, *L52* and *L22*. For one shilling (5p) admission visitors could see HMS *Hood*, *Warspite*, *Renown*, and the aircraft carrier *Courageous*. HMS *Nelson* was in dry dock, and the visitors could walk in the shadow of her huge hull. Five hundred hikers descended on the city for the event, and many camped on Portsdown Hill. One man walked all the way from Leith in Scotland, taking a fortnight to complete the trip.

Navy Weeks were popular with families but they also served as a showcase to attract would-be sailors. The souvenir programmes were always illustrated with stirring or ceremonial scenes, as is this issue from August 1935.

HMS *Suffolk* is welcomed as she comes alongside for Navy Week in August 1935. The Kent class cruiser was the fifth to bear the name, and was built in Portsmouth dockyard. She was launched with due ceremony on 16 February 1926 by the Marchioness of Bristol, when it took six attempts to break the champagne bottle on her bows.

On 12 June 1934, the 7000-ton cruiser HMS *Amphion* was launched in Portsmouth dockyard. The ceremony was performed by the Marchioness of Titchfield, who broke a bottle of empire wine across her bows.

The wife of Captain H.D. Bridges of HMS *Vernon* lays the keel plate for *Nightingale*, the new mining school tender, on 12 September 1930. This was part of a triple ceremony in the dockyard, in which keel plates were also laid for the destroyers *Crusader* and *Comet*. Lady Keyes, wife of the commander-in-chief, Admiral Sir Roger Keyes, laid the *Crusader* keel, while Mrs Donaldson, wife of Vice Admiral L.A.B. Donaldson, did the honours for *Comet*.

On 12 June 1934 the United States cruiser USS *New Orleans* paid a visit to the dockyard. The huge vessel was the first of the new Astoria class ships, and had been built at the New York navy yards. She is seen here alongside at Portsmouth with her complement of two Curtis Seagull aircraft.

Here the dockyard gates are decorated for the silver jubilee of George V and Queen Mary in May 1935. A huge congregation attended a thanksgiving service held in the Guildhall Square, and in the evening a beacon was lit on Portsdown Hill, one of a chain of such fires running around Britain's coastline. (*The News*, Portsmouth)

Patriotic feeling was high between the wars, as shown by this picture of one of Portsmouth's poorer streets, with simple bunting and decorations strung out to celebrate the silver jubilee. Father Frederick Dolling's church of St Agatha can be glimpsed in the background, which identifies the location as Trafalgar Street. The street is long gone, but St Agatha's still stands.

On 15 July 1935 George V visited Portsmouth for the jubilee review of the fleet, a line of ships stretching for 27 miles. In attendance was the royal yacht *Victoria and Albert*, pictured here in the harbour waiting to proceed to Spithead.

A winter scene in 1929 as skaters take to the frozen Hilsea moat. The corporation records for the year noted: 'Portsmouth, in common with the rest of the country experienced Arctic conditions of weather in February. On the 13th, 22 degrees of frost were registered, the Canoe Lake and moats were frozen, and skating was general in the district. On the night of the 14th, 25 degrees of frost were registered, this being the worst ever officially recorded in Portsmouth.'

The Bastion tearooms at Hilsea can be seen in the distance in this unusual scene. The sheer weight of ice has pulled the telegraph and telephone wires down to ground level, giving the impression of some strange work of modern art.

A well-wrapped-up nanny and her two charges wait to cross the road outside the Parade Hotel at a snow-covered Western Parade, Southsea, in January 1929.

Two postmen pull up the collars of their greatcoats and push their cold hands deep into their pockets as they make their way across Victoria Park during the same bitter winter of 1929. Behind them the waters of the fountain hang in long icicles, and the pond itself is frozen solid.

A period of unusually heavy rain made this area of North End a quagmire in 1930. The unfinished roads around Madeira Road formed an obstacle course for residents. Even motorists were not immune, as this driver found to his cost.

Looking towards to North End junction in 1929: the top deck of a tram proved a good vantage point for this enterprising photographer. On the far right can be seen the back of a tram going in the opposite direction – one of a batch of twelve closed-top vehicles that began service in 1920.

The foreshore at Stamshaw was a popular place to walk. Today the M275 dominates the horizon but the mud flats and little fishing boats remain, an echo of the 1920s and 1930s.

The old lamplighter's cottage at Cosham in December 1930, later demolished to make way for modern housing development.

The tea lawns at the Hilsea Bastion on a summer's day. A three-piece band – drums, piano, and banjo – plays in the tiny bandstand, as one daring couple trip the light fantastic on the grass.

With the increasing construction of housing in the northern part of the city, the Hilsea Lido and gardens were opened. The promenade around the lido area was a popular place for a stroll. (*The News*, Portsmouth)

87

Work is is full swing at Portsmouth's municipal kitchen in Heidelberg Road, Southsea, at Christmas 1931. The food was distributed by the lord mayor and lady mayoress during their annual goodwill tour of the city's poorer areas, along with toys and gifts from the lady mayoress's Santa Claus appeal.

Senior members of the Independent Order of Rechabites celebrate the opening of their new hall at Southsea on the corner of Victoria Road North and Britannia Road. (The building still stands.) A temperance friendly society which started in Salford, Lancashire, in 1835, the order organised help and sick payments for its members, who had to abide by its no-drink rules. It was named after the nomadic tribe of Rechab (Jeremiah 35), who swore to take no wine.

Two French airliners pay an unexpected visit to Portsmouth airport in September 1933. Opened the previous year, the airport promised great things for the city.

It is dawn on 9 September 1936, and the aircraft competing in the South Africa air race line up for take-off at Portsmouth airport under the harsh glare of floodlights. The South African magnate L.W. Schlesinger had put up the £10,000 prize money, and Portsmouth airport was chosen for the start because of its excellent grass surface. The race was won by C.W.A. Scott and Giles Guthrie in a Percival Vega Gull in 52 hours, 56 minutes. The Portsmouth-built Airspeed Envoy, number 13 in the starting order, crashed at Broken Hill, killing the pilot, Captain Maxwell Findlay, and his radio operator, A.H. Morgan.

The long white marquees and tents of the Royal Counties Agricultural Show form geometric patterns on Southsea Common in this aerial photograph taken in 1939. It was the eighth time this popular event had been held on the common, and it ran from 31 May to 3 June. The king's birthday parade on 8 June 1939 had to be moved to Fort Grange aerodrome at Gosport because of the show.

Prize animals are led around the show ring at the agricultural show. Although the weather was remarkably fine, the attendance was only 61,000 and did not reach, as had been hoped, the record 1925 figure of 79,000. The council's total profit from the show was £1,584.

Arundel Street public market hall opened in November 1932 – just in time for Christmas. Considered to be a most up-to-date shopping centre, it had electric light, hot and cold water, and all modern conveniences.

A peaceful view of tree-lined Stubbington Avenue, North End, with its elegant and substantial Edwardian homes. Much of the area was formerly farmland surrounding the long-gone Stubbington Lodge.

Tram 22 passes Mile End cemetery, an area now totally taken over by the city's continental ferry port. Pylo's shop offers a plea for National Bike Week. The cemetery, with its line of pillars, was levelled in the 1950s and turned into a public park. There were hopes of retaining the colonnade, but an architect's report advised that repairs and renovation would be too costly. (Tom Dethridge)

Parents watch their offspring take to the miniature railway at Southsea in 1939, the last peacetime summer before the war. Opened in 1924, the track was three-quarters of a mile long, and the engines ran on a $9^{1}/_{2}$-inch-gauge layout. The line boasted a turntable, engine shed, two locomotives, and a tunnel!

Workers of both sexes gather outside the offices of the *Evening News* in Stanhope Road on 3 September 1939 – the day war with Germany was declared – anxiously reading hot-off-the-press copies of the special Sunday edition. The balmy days of the 1920s and 1930s had come to an abrupt end, and life for the majority of British people would never be the same again. (*The News*, Portsmouth)

About the Author

Anthony Triggs is the author of seven previous books on the history of the Portsmouth area. He is a sub-editor with *The News*, Portsmouth, and lives at Portchester with his wife Sue. In addition to local history Anthony lists his interests as family history, photography, and the Sherlock Holmes stories.